NORTH CAROLINA GENERAL STATUTES
2019 EDITION

BOATING SAFETY ACT

Revised on June 8, 2019 by West Hartford Legal Publishing

NORTH CAROLINA LEGISLATURE

Contents

Chapter 75A.
Boating and Water Safety.

Article 1. Boating Safety Act.

§ 75A-1. Declaration of policy.

It is the policy of this State to promote safety for persons and property in and connected with the use, operation, and equipment of vessels, and to promote uniformity of laws relating thereto. (1959, c. 1064, s. 1.)

§ 75A-2. Definitions.

As used in this Chapter, unless the context clearly requires a different meaning:

(1) "Abandoned vessel" means a vessel that has been relinquished, left, or given up by the lawful owner without the intention to later resume any right or interest in the vessel. The term does not include a vessel that is left by an owner or agent of the owner with any person or business for the purpose of storage, maintenance, or repair and that is not subsequently reclaimed.

(1a) "Certificate of number" means the document and permanent identification number issued by the Wildlife Resources Commission for the purpose of registering a vessel in this State.

(1b) "Commission" means the Wildlife Resources Commission.

(1c) "Director" means the Executive Director of the Wildlife Resources Commission.

(1d)   "Electric generating facility" means any plant facilities and equipment used for the purposes of producing, generating, transmitting, delivering, or furnishing electricity for the production of power.

(1e)   "Motorboat" means any vessel equipped with propulsion machinery of any type, whether or not the machinery is the principal source of propulsion: Provided, that "propulsion machinery" as used in this section shall not include an electric motor when used as the only means of mechanical propulsion of any vessel.

(1f)   "No-wake speed" means idle speed or slow speed creating no appreciable wake.

(2)   "Operate" means to navigate or otherwise use or occupy any motorboat or vessel that is afloat.

(3)   "Owner" means a person, other than a lienholder, having the property in or title to a vessel. The term includes a person entitled to the use or possession of a vessel subject to an interest in another person, reserved or created by agreement and securing payment or performance of an obligation, but the term excludes a lessee under a lease not intended as security.

(4)   "Person" means an individual, partnership, firm, corporation, association, or other entity.

(4a)   "Underway" means a vessel that is not at anchor, or made fast to the shore, or aground.

(5)   "Vessel" means every description of watercraft or structure, other than a seaplane on the water, used or capable of being used as a means of transportation or habitation on the water.

(6)   "Waters of this State" means any waters within the territorial limits of this State, and the marginal sea adjacent to this State and the high seas when navigated as a part of a journey or ride to or from the shore of this State, but does not include private ponds as defined in G.S. 113-129.

(7)   Redesignated as subdivision (1d). (1959, c. 1064, s. 2; 1965, c. 634, s. 1; 1969, c. 87; 1975, c. 340, s. 1; 1983, c. 446, s. 1; 1993 (Reg. Sess., 1994), c. 753, s. 2; 2006-185, s. 1.)

§ 75A-3. Wildlife Resources Commission to administer Chapter; Boating Safety Committee; funds for administration.

(a)   The Commission shall enforce and administer the provisions of this Chapter.

(b)   The chair of the Commission shall designate from among the members of the Commission three members who shall serve as the Boating Safety Committee of the Commission, and who shall, in their activities with the Commission, place special emphasis on the administration and enforcement of this Chapter.

(c)   The Boating Account is established within the Wildlife Resources Fund created under G.S. 143-250. Interest and other investment income earned by the Account accrues to the Account. All moneys collected pursuant to the numbering and titling provisions of this Chapter shall be credited to this Account. Motor fuel excise tax revenue is credited to the Account under G.S. 105-449.126. The Commission shall use revenue in the Account, subject to the Executive Budget Act and the Personnel Act, for the administration and enforcement of this Chapter; for activities relating to boating and water safety including education and waterway marking and improvement; and for boating access area acquisition, development, and maintenance. The Commission shall use at least three dollars ($3.00) of each one-year certificate of number fee and at least nine dollars ($9.00) of each three-year certificate of number fee collected under the numbering provisions of G.S. 75A-5 for boating access area acquisition, development, and maintenance. The Commission shall transfer on a quarterly basis fifty percent (50%) of each one-year certificate of number fee and fifty percent (50%) of each three-year certificate of number fee collected under the numbering provisions of G.S. 75A-5 to the Shallow Draft Navigation Channel Dredging and Aquatic Weed Fund established by G.S. 143-215.73F. (1959, c. 1064, s. 3; 1961, c. 644; 1963, c. 1003; 1981 (Reg. Sess., 1982), c. 1182, s. 2; 1993, c. 422, s. 1; 1995, c. 390, s. 13; 1999-392, s. 5; 2006-185, s. 1; 2007-485, s. 4.1; 2013-360, s. 14.22(a); 2013-380, s. 3; 2014-100, s. 14.19(b); 2016-94, s. 14.12(b).)

§ 75A-4. Identification numbers required.

Every vessel on the waters of this State shall be numbered, except those vessels exempted from numbering under G.S. 75A-7. No person shall operate or give permission for the operation of any vessel on the waters of this State unless all of the following conditions are met:

(1)   The vessel is numbered in accordance with this Chapter, or in accordance with applicable federal law, or in accordance with a federally approved numbering system of another state.

(2)   The certificate of number awarded to the vessel is in full force and effect.

(3)   The identification number set forth in the certificate of number is displayed on each side of the bow of the vessel. (1959, c. 1064, s. 4; 1983, c. 446, s. 1; 1999-392, s. 1; 2006-185, s. 1.)

§ 75A-5. Application for certificate of number; fees; reciprocity; change of ownership; conformity with federal regulations; records; award of certificates; renewal of certificates; transfer of partial interest; destroyed or junked vessels; abandonment; change of address; duplicate certificates; display.

(a)	Application for Certificate of Number. - The owner of each vessel requiring numbering by this State shall file an application for a certificate of number with the Commission. The Commission shall furnish application forms and shall prescribe the information contained in the application form. The application shall be signed by the owner of the vessel or the owner's agent and shall be accompanied by a fee, as set out in subsection (a1) of this section. The fee does not apply to vessels owned and operated by nonprofit rescue squads if they are operated exclusively for rescue purposes, including rescue training. The owner shall have the option of selecting a one-year numbering period or a three-year numbering period. Upon receipt of the application in approved form, the Commission shall enter the application in its records and issue the owner a certificate of number stating the identification number awarded to the vessel and the name and address of the owner, and a validation decal indicating the expiration date of the certificate of number. The owner shall paint on or attach to each side of the bow of the vessel the identification number in such manner as may be prescribed by rules of the Commission in order that it may be clearly visible. The identification number shall be maintained in legible condition. The validation decal shall be displayed on the starboard bow of the vessel immediately following the number. The certificate of number shall be pocket size and shall be available for inspection on the vessel for which the certificate is issued at all times the vessel is in operation. Any person charged with failing to so carry a certificate of number shall not be convicted if the person produces in court a certificate of number previously issued to the owner that was valid at the time of the alleged violation.

(a1)   Fees. - The fees for certificates of number are as set out in this subsection:

- (1)   The fee for a certificate of number for a one-year period is:
  - a.   Thirty dollars ($30.00) for a vessel that is less than 26 feet in length.
  - b.   Fifty dollars ($50.00) for a vessel that is 26 feet or more in length.
- (2)   The fee for a certificate of number for a three-year period is:
  - a.   Ninety dollars ($90.00) for a vessel that is less than 26 feet in length.
  - b.   One hundred fifty dollars ($150.00) for a vessel that is 26 feet or more in length.

(b)   Reciprocity. - The owner of any vessel already covered by a number in full force and effect pursuant to federal law or a federally approved numbering system of another state shall record the identification number prior to operating the vessel on the waters of this State in excess of the 90-day reciprocity period provided for in G.S. 75A-7(a)(1). The recordation shall be made pursuant to subsection (a) of this section, except that no additional or substitute identification number shall be issued.

(c)   Change of Ownership. - Should the ownership of a vessel change, a new application form with a fee in the amount set in subsection (a) of this section shall be filed with the Commission and a new certificate bearing the same identification number shall be awarded to the new owner in the same manner as an original certificate of number. Possession of the certificate shall in cases involving prosecution for violation of any provision of this Chapter be prima facie evidence that the person whose name appears on the certificate is the owner of the vessel referred to on the certificate.

(d)　　Conformity With Federal Regulations. - In the event that an agency of the federal government shall have in force an over-all system of identification numbering for vessels within the United States, the numbering system employed pursuant to this Chapter by the Commission shall be in conformity therewith.

(e)　　Repealed by Session Laws 2006-185, s. 1.

(f)　　Records. - All records of the Commission made or kept pursuant to this section shall be public records.

(g)　　Award of Certificates. - Each certificate of number awarded pursuant to this Chapter, unless sooner terminated or discontinued in accordance with the provisions of this Chapter, shall continue in full force and effect to and including the last day of the month during which the certificate was awarded after the lapse of one year in the case of a one-year certificate or three years in the case of a three-year certificate. No person shall willfully remove a validation decal from any vessel during the continuance of its validity or alter, counterfeit, or otherwise tamper with a validation decal attached to any vessel for the purpose of changing or obscuring the indicated date of expiration of the certificate of number of the vessel.

(h)　　Renewal of Certificates. - An owner of a vessel awarded a certificate of number pursuant to this Chapter shall renew the certificate on or before the first day of the month after which the certificate expires; otherwise, the certificate shall lapse and be void until such time as it may thereafter be renewed. Application for renewal shall be submitted on a form approved by the Commission and shall be accompanied by a fee in the amount set in subsection (a1) of this section.

(i)   Transfer of Partial Interest. - The owner shall furnish the Commission notice of the transfer of any part of the owner's interest other than the creation of a security interest in a vessel numbered in this State pursuant to subsections (a) and (b) of this section within 15 days of the transfer. A transfer of partial interest in a vessel shall not affect the owner's right to operate the vessel, nor shall a transfer of partial interest in a vessel terminate the certificate of number.

(i1)   Destroyed or Junked Vessels. - The owner of any destroyed or junked vessel shall furnish the Commission notice of the destruction or junking of that vessel within 15 days of its occurrence. Destruction or junking terminates the certificate of number and renders the hull identification number invalid for that vessel.

(i2)   Abandonment. - A person may acquire ownership of an abandoned vessel by providing proof to the Commission that the lawful owner has actually abandoned the vessel. The Commission shall adopt rules by which a person seeking to acquire ownership may demonstrate that the vessel is actually abandoned. At a minimum, the rules shall provide for a reasonable attempt to locate the lawful owner and, if the owner is located, notice by the claimant of an intention to claim ownership of the vessel.

(j)   Change of Address. - Whenever any person, after applying for or obtaining the certificate of number of a vessel, moves from the address shown in the application or upon the certificate of number, that person shall notify the Commission of the change of address within 30 days of moving in a form acceptable to the Commission.

(j1)   Duplicate Certificates. - The Commission shall issue a duplicate certificate of number for a vessel upon application by the person entitled to hold the certificate, if the Commission is satisfied that the original certificate of number has been lost, stolen, mutilated, or destroyed, or has become illegible. The Commission shall charge a fee of five dollars ($5.00) for issuance of each duplicate certificate.

(k)   Display. - No number other than the identification number set forth in the certificate of number or granted reciprocity pursuant to this Chapter shall be painted, attached, or otherwise displayed on either side of the bow of a vessel, except the validation decal required by subsection (a) of this section.

(l)   Repealed by Session Laws 2006-185, s. 1. (1959, c. 1064, s. 5; 1961, c. 469, s. 1; 1963, c. 470; 1975, c. 483, ss. 1, 2; 1977, c. 566; 1979, c. 761, ss. 1-7; 1981, c. 161; 1983, c. 194; c. 446, ss. 1, 2; 1987, c. 827, s. 4; 1993, c. 422, ss. 2-4; c. 539, ss. 563, 564; 1994, Ex. Sess., c. 24, s. 14(c); 1998-225, s. 4.1; 1999-248, ss. 1, 2; 1999-392, ss. 2-4; 2006-185, s. 1; 2007-485, ss. 4.2, 4.3, 4.4; 2013-360, s. 14.22(b).)

§ 75A-5.1: Repealed by Session Laws 2013-360, s. 14.22(c), effective October 1, 2013.

§ 75A-5.2. Vessel agents.

(a)   In order to facilitate the convenience of the public, the efficiency of administration, the need to keep statistics and records affecting the conservation of wildlife resources, boating, water safety, and other matters within the jurisdiction of the Commission, and to facilitate vessel transactions, the Commission may conduct vessel transactions through any of the following:

(1)   Vessel agents.

(2)   The Commission's headquarters.

(3)   Employees of the Commission.

(4)   Two or more of those sources simultaneously.

(b)   When there are substantial reasons for differing treatment, the Commission may conduct vessel transactions by one method in one locality and by another method in another locality.

(c)   As compensation for services rendered to the Commission and to the general public, vessel agents shall receive the surcharge listed below. The surcharge shall be added to the fee for each certificate issued.

(1)   Renewal of certificate of number - $3.00.

(2)   Transfer of ownership and certificate of number - $5.00.

(3)   Issuance of new certificate of number - $5.00.

(4)   Issuance of duplicate certificate of number - $3.00.

(5)   Issuance or transfer of certificate of title - $5.00.

(d)   When certificates of number are to be issued by vessel agents as provided by subsection (a) of this section, the Commission may adopt rules to provide for any of the following:

(1)   Qualifications of the vessel agents.

(2)   Duties of the vessel agents.

(3)   Methods and procedures to ensure accountability and security for proceeds and unissued certificates of number.

(4)   Types and amounts of evidence that a vessel agent must submit to relieve the agent of responsibility for losses due to occurrences beyond the control of the agent.

(5)   Any other reasonable requirement or condition that the Commission deems necessary to expedite and

control the issuance of certificates of number by vessel agents.

(e)   The Commission may adopt rules to authorize the Director to take any of the following actions related to vessel agents:

(1)   Select and appoint vessel agents in the areas most convenient to the boating public.

(2)   Limit the number of vessel agents in any one area if necessary for efficiency of operation.

(3)   Require prompt and accurate reporting and remittance of public funds or documents by vessel agents.

(4)   Conduct periodic and special audits of accounts.

(5)   Suspend or terminate the authorization of any vessel agent found to be noncompliant with rules adopted by the Commission or when State funds or property are reasonably believed to be in jeopardy.

(6)   Require the immediate surrender of all equipment, forms, supplies, records, and State funds and property issued by or belonging to the Commission, in the event of the termination of a license agent.

(f)   The Commission is exempt from the contested case provisions of Chapter 150B of the General Statutes with respect to determinations of whether to authorize or terminate the authority of a person to conduct vessel transactions as a vessel agent of the Commission.

(g)   If any check or bank account draft of any vessel agent for the issuance of certificates of number shall be returned by the banking facility upon which the same is drawn for lack of funds, the vessel agent shall be liable to the Commission for a penalty of five percent (5%) of the amount of the check or bank account draft, but in no event shall the penalty be less than five dollars ($5.00) or more than two hundred dollars ($200.00). Vessel agents shall be assessed a penalty of twenty-five percent (25%) of their issuing fee on all remittances to the Commission after the fifteenth day of the month immediately following the month of sale.

(h)   It is a Class 1 misdemeanor for a vessel agent to do any of the following:

  (1)   Withhold or misappropriate funds generated from vessel transactions.

  (2)   Falsify records of vessel transactions.

  (3)   Willfully and knowingly assist or allow a person to obtain a certificate of number or certificate of title for which the person is ineligible.

  (4)   Willfully issue a backdated certificate of number or certificate of title.

  (5)   Willfully include false information or omit material information on vessel transaction forms and records regarding either:

    a.   A person's entitlement to a particular certificate of number or certificate of title.

    b.   The applicability or term of a particular certificate of number.

  (6)   Charge or accept any fee, remuneration, or other item of value that exceeds the fee amounts provided by statute.

  (7)   Charge or accept any additional fee, remuneration, or other item of value in association with any activity set out in subdivisions (1) through (5) of this subsection. (2006-185, s. 1; 2013-283, s. 17.)

§ 75A-6. Classification; rules.

(a)   Vessels subject to the provisions of this Chapter shall be divided into five categories as follows:

   (1) Class A. Less than 16 feet in length.

   (2) Class 1. Sixteen feet or over and less than 26 feet in length.

   (3) Class 2. Twenty-six feet or over and less than 40 feet in length.

   (4) Class 3. Forty feet or over and not more than 65 feet in length.

   (5) Class 4. More than 65 feet in length.

(b)   through (e) Repealed by Session Laws 1993, c. 361, s. 2.

(f)   through (j) Repealed by Session Laws 2006-185, s. 1.

(k)   Repealed by Session Laws 1993, c. 361, s. 2.

(l)   No person shall operate or give permission for the operation of a vessel that is not equipped as required by this section.

(m)   The Commission may adopt rules to conform to the Federal Boat Safety Act of 1971 and the federal regulations adopted pursuant thereto.

(n)   All vessels propelled by machinery of 10 hp or less that are operated on the public waters of this State shall carry at least one personal flotation device, life belt, ring buoy, or other device of the sort prescribed by rules of the Commission for each person on board, and from one-half hour after sunset to one-half hour before sunrise shall carry a white light in the stern or shall have on board a hand flashlight in good working condition, which light shall be ready at hand and shall be temporarily displayed in sufficient time to prevent collision.

(o)   The Commission for Public Health shall adopt rules establishing standards for sewage treatment devices and holding tanks for marine toilets installed in vessels operating on the inland fishing waters of the State as designated by the Commission and the inland lake waters of the State. The Commission shall not issue a certificate of number for any vessel operating on the inland fishing waters of the State as designated by the Commission and the inland lake waters of this State that is equipped with a marine toilet unless the vessel is provided with a sewage treatment device or holding tank approved by the Commission for Public Health. All vessels operating on the inland fishing waters of the State as designated by the Commission and the inland lake waters of the State that are equipped with a marine toilet shall provide a sewage treatment device or holding tank approved by the Commission for Public Health. Wildlife protectors may inspect vessels on the inland fishing waters of the State as designated by the Commission and the inland lake waters to determine if approved treatment devices or holding tanks are properly installed and if they are operating in a satisfactory manner. A vessel registered, documented, or otherwise licensed in another state and equipped with a marine toilet not prohibited in such state may be operated on the inland fishing waters of the State as designated by the Commission, without regard to the provisions of this subsection while making an interstate trip. (1959, c. 1064, s. 6; 1963, c. 396; 1965, c. 634, s. 2; 1967, cc. 230, 1075; 1971, c. 296, ss. 1, 2; 1973, c. 476, s. 128; 1975, c. 340, s. 2; c. 483, s. 3; 1989 (Reg. Sess., 1990), c. 1004, s. 55; 1993, c. 361, s. 2; 2006-185, s. 1; 2007-182, s. 2.)

§ 75A-6.1. Navigation rules.

(a)   Every vessel operated on the waters of this State that is required to obtain an identification number pursuant to this

Chapter, has a valid marine document issued by the federal Bureau of Customs or any federal agency successor to it, or issued pursuant to a federally approved numbering system of another state shall comply with the navigation rules, including requirements for navigational lights, sound-signaling devices, and other equipment, contained in the Inland Navigational Rules Act of 1980, codified as amended at 33 U.S.C. §§ 2001-2038, 2071-2073 (1993) and rules adopted pursuant thereto, see 33 C.F.R. Part 84 (1992).

(b)   The Commission is responsible for the enforcement of the rules specified in subsection (a) of this section. The rules specified in subsection (a) of this section are also enforceable by all peace officers with general subject matter jurisdiction.

(c)   Violation of any rule governing navigational lighting adopted by the Commission shall constitute an infraction as provided in G.S. 14-3.1. (1993, c. 361, s. 1; 1994, Ex. Sess., c. 14, s. 44; 2006-185, s. 1; 2013-360, s. 18B.15(a); 2013-380, s. 4.)

§ 75A-7. Exemption from numbering requirements.

(a)   A vessel shall not be required to be numbered under this Chapter if it is:

    (1)   A vessel that is required to be awarded an identification number pursuant to federal law or a federally approved numbering system of another state, and for which an identification number has been so awarded: Provided, that any such vessel shall not have been within this State for a period in excess of 90 consecutive days.

    (2)   A vessel from a country other than the United States temporarily using the waters of this State.

(3)   A vessel whose owner is the United States, a state or a subdivision thereof.

(4)   A ship's lifeboat.

(5)   Repealed by Session Laws 2013-360, s. 14.22(d), effective October 1, 2013.

(6)   A sailboat of not more than 14 feet on the load water line (LWL).

(7)   A vessel with no means of propulsion other than drifting or manual paddling, poling, or rowing.

(b)   The Commission is hereby empowered to permit the voluntary numbering of vessels owned by the United States, a state or a subdivision thereof.

(c)   Those vessels owned by the United States, a state or a subdivision thereof and those owned by nonprofit rescue squads may be assigned a certificate of number bearing no expiration date but which shall be stamped with the word "permanent" and shall not be renewable so long as the vessel remains the property of the governmental entity or nonprofit rescue squad. If the ownership of any such vessel is transferred from one governmental entity to another or to a nonprofit rescue squad or if a vessel owned by a nonprofit rescue squad is transferred to another nonprofit rescue squad or governmental entity, the Commission shall issue a new permanent certificate of number, displaying the same identification number, without charge to the successor entity. When any such vessel is sold to a private owner or is otherwise transferred to private ownership, the applicable certificate of number shall be deemed to have expired immediately prior to the transfer. Prior to further use on the waters of this State, the new owner shall obtain a certificate of number pursuant to the provisions of this Chapter. The provisions of this subsection applicable to a vessel owned by a nonprofit rescue squad apply only to a vessel operated exclusively for rescue purposes, including rescue training. (1959, c. 1064, s. 7; 1981, c. 162; 1983, c. 446, ss. 1-3; 2006-185, s. 1; 2013-360, s. 14.22(d).)

§ 75A-8. Vessel liveries.

An owner of a vessel livery shall not rent a vessel to any person unless the provisions of this Chapter have been complied with. An owner of a vessel livery shall equip all vessels rented as required by this Chapter. (1959, c. 1064, s. 8; 1975, c. 340, s. 3; 1983, c. 446, s. 1; 2006-185, s. 1.)

§ 75A-9. Muffling devices.

(a)   Every internal combustion engine used on a vessel shall have effective muffling equipment installed and used on the exhaust to muffle the noise in a reasonable manner. The use of cutouts is prohibited.

(b)   Every internal combustion engine with an open-air exhaust that is used on a vessel that has a capacity of operating at more than 4,000 revolutions per minute shall have effective muffling equipment installed and used on each exhaust manifold stack. This subsection shall not apply to a licensed commercial fishing vessel.

(c)   This section shall not apply to vessels competing in a regatta or race approved by the United States Coast Guard, for such vessels while on trial runs during a period not to exceed 48 hours immediately preceding the regatta or race, and for such vessels while competing in official trials for speed records during a period not to exceed 48 hours immediately following the regatta or race. (1959, c. 1064, s. 9; 2006-185, s. 1.)

§ 75A-9.1: Repealed by Session Laws 2006-185, s. 1, effective January 1, 2007, and applicable to offenses committed on or after January 1, 2007.

§ 75A-10. Operating vessel or manipulating water skis, etc., in reckless manner; operating, etc., while intoxicated, etc.; depositing or discharging litter, etc.

(a)   No person shall operate any motorboat or vessel, or manipulate any water skis, surfboard, or similar device on the waters of this State in a reckless or negligent manner so as to endanger the life, limb, or property of any person.

(b)   No person shall manipulate any water skis, surfboard, nonmotorized vessel, or similar device on the waters of this State while under the influence of an impairing substance.

(b1)   No person shall operate any vessel while underway on the waters of this State:

      (1)   While under the influence of an impairing substance, or

      (2)   After having consumed sufficient alcohol that the person has, at any relevant time after the boating, an alcohol concentration of 0.08 or more.

(b2)   The fact that a person charged with violating this subsection is or has been legally entitled to use alcohol or a drug is not a defense to a charge under subsections (b) and (b1) of this section. The relevant definitions contained in G.S. 20-4.01 shall apply to subsections (b), (b1), and (b2) of this section.

(b3)   A person who violates a provision of subsection (a) or (b) of this section is guilty of a Class 2 misdemeanor.

(b4)   A person who violates subsection (b1) of this section is guilty of a Class 2 misdemeanor, and upon conviction, in addition to any other penalty imposed, shall be fined not less than two hundred fifty dollars ($250.00).

(c)   No person shall place, throw, deposit, or discharge or cause to be placed, thrown, deposited, or discharged on the waters of this State or into the inland lake waters of this State, any litter, raw sewage, bottles, cans, papers, or other liquid or solid materials which render the waters unsightly, noxious, or otherwise unwholesome so as to be detrimental to the public health or welfare or to the enjoyment and safety of the water for recreational purposes.

(d)   No person shall place, throw, deposit, or discharge or cause to be placed, thrown, deposited, or discharged on the waters of this State or into the inland lake waters of this State any medical waste as defined by G.S. 130A-290 which renders the waters unsightly, noxious, or otherwise unwholesome so as to be detrimental to the public health or welfare or to the enjoyment and safety of the water for recreational purposes.

(e)   A person who willfully violates subsection (d) of this section is guilty of a Class 1 misdemeanor. A person who willfully violates subsection (d) of this section and in so doing releases medical waste that creates a substantial risk of physical injury to any person who is not a participant in the offense is guilty of a Class F felony which may include a fine not to exceed fifty thousand dollars ($50,000) per day of violation. (1959, c. 1064, s. 10; 1965, c. 634, s. 3; 1985, c. 615, ss. 1-5; 1989, c. 742, s. 1; 1995, c. 506, s. 14; 2006-185, s. 1; 2013-380, s. 5; 2016-34, s. 3.)

§ 75A-10.1. Family purpose doctrine applicable.

The family purpose doctrine, as applicable in this State to tort cases arising from the operation of motor vehicles, shall apply to tort cases arising from the operation of motorboats and vessels as those terms are defined in this Chapter. (1971, c. 450, s. 1.)

§ 75A-10.2. Proof of ownership of a vessel.

(a)   In all actions to recover damages for injury to the person or to property or for the death of a person, arising out of an accident or collision involving a vessel, proof of ownership of such vessel at the time of the accident or collision shall be prima facie evidence that the vessel was being operated and used with the authority, consent and knowledge of the owner in the very transaction out of which the injury or cause of action arose.

(b)   Proof of the certificate of number stating the identification number awarded to the vessel in the name of any person, firm, or corporation as required by this Chapter, or proof of the licensing, registration, or documentation of the vessel as required by other state or federal law in the name of any person, firm, or corporation, shall for the purpose of any such action, be prima facie evidence of ownership and that the vessel was then being operated by and under the control of a person for whose conduct the owner was legally responsible, for the owner's benefit, and within the course and scope of the operator's employment. (1971, c. 652, s. 1; 2006-185, s. 1.)

§ 75A-10.3. Death or serious injury by impaired boating; repeat offenses.

(a)   Death by Impaired Boating. - A person commits the offense of death by impaired boating if all of the following apply:

    (1)   The person unintentionally causes the death of another person.

(2)   The person was engaged in the offense of impaired boating under G.S. 75A-10(b1).

(3)   The commission of the offense in subdivision (2) of this subsection is the proximate cause of the death.

(b)   Serious Injury by Impaired Boating. - A person commits the offense of serious injury by impaired boating if all of the following apply:

(1)   The person unintentionally causes serious injury to another person.

(2)   The person was engaged in the offense of impaired boating under G.S. 75A-10(b1).

(3)   The commission of the offense in subdivision (2) of this subsection is the proximate cause of the serious injury.

(c)   Aggravated Serious Injury by Impaired Boating. - A person commits the offense of aggravated serious injury by impaired boating if all of the following apply:

(1)   The person unintentionally causes serious injury to another person.

(2)   The person was engaged in the offense of impaired boating under G.S. 75A-10(b1).

(3)   The commission of the offense in subdivision (2) of this subsection is the proximate cause of the serious injury.

(4)   The person has a previous conviction of impaired boating under G.S. 75A-10(b1) within seven years of the date of the offense.

(d)   Aggravated Death by Impaired Boating. - A person commits the offense of aggravated death by impaired boating if all of the following apply:

(1) The person unintentionally causes the death of another person.

(2) The person was engaged in the offense of impaired boating under G.S. 75A-10(b1).

(3) The commission of the offense in subdivision (2) of this subsection is the proximate cause of the death.

(4) The person has a previous conviction of impaired boating under G.S. 75A-10(b1) within seven years of the date of the offense.

(e) Repeat Death by Impaired Boating. - A person commits the offense of repeat death by impaired boating if all of the following apply:

(1) The person commits an offense under subsection (a) or subsection (d) of this section.

(2) The person has a previous conviction under at least one of the following:

a. Subsection (a) of this section.

b. Subsection (d) of this section.

c. G.S. 14-17 or G.S. 14-18, and the basis of the conviction was the unintentional death of another person while engaged in the offense of impaired boating under G.S. 75A-10(b1).

The pleading and proof of previous convictions shall be in accordance with the provisions of G.S. 15A-928.

(f) Punishments. - Unless the conduct is covered under some other provision of law providing greater punishment, the following classifications apply to the offenses set forth in this section:

(1) Repeat death by impaired boating is a Class B2 felony.

(2)   Aggravated death by impaired boating is a Class D felony. Notwithstanding the provisions of G.S. 15A-1340.17, the court shall sentence the defendant in the aggravated range of the appropriate Prior Record Level.

(3)   Death by impaired boating is a Class D felony. Notwithstanding the provisions of G.S. 15A-1340.17, intermediate punishment is authorized for a defendant who is a Prior Record Level I offender.

(4)   Aggravated serious injury by impaired boating is a Class E felony.

(5)   Serious injury by impaired boating is a Class F felony.

(g)   No Double Prosecutions. - No person who has been placed in jeopardy upon a charge of death by impaired boating may be prosecuted for the offense of manslaughter arising out of the same death; and no person who has been placed in jeopardy upon a charge of manslaughter may be prosecuted for death by impaired boating arising out of the same death. (2016-34, s. 2.)

§ 75A-11. Duty of operator involved in collision, accident, casualty, or other occurrence.

(a)   For the purposes of this section, the term "occurrence" means a collision, accident, casualty, or other similar occurrence involving a vessel. The operator of a vessel involved in an occurrence, so far as the operator is able to do so without serious danger to the operator's vessel, crew, and passengers (if any), shall render persons affected by the occurrence any assistance as may be practicable and necessary in order to save them from or minimize any danger caused by the occurrence, and also to give the operator's name, address, and identification of the operator's vessel in writing to any person injured and to the owner of any property damaged in the occurrence.

(b)   If an occurrence results in the death, injury, or disappearance indicating death or injury of a person or damage to a vessel or other property of two thousand dollars ($2,000) or more, or if there is complete loss of any vessel, the operator of the vessel shall file with the Commission a full description of the occurrence, including any information the agency may, by rule, require. If an occurrence results in death, disappearance, or injury, the operator of the vessel shall file the report with the Commission within 48 hours of the occurrence. If the occurrence results in vessel or property damage, or complete loss of any vessel, the operator of the vessel shall file the report with the Commission within 10 days of the occurrence. When the operator of the vessel cannot submit the report, the owner of the vessel shall submit the report. Reports filed pursuant to this subsection shall not be admissible as evidence.

(c)   When, as a result of an occurrence that involves a vessel or its equipment, a person dies or disappears from a vessel, the operator of the vessel shall, without delay and by the most expeditious means available, notify the nearest law enforcement agency of all of the following:

(1)   The date, time, and exact location of the occurrence.
(2)   The name of each person who died or disappeared.
(3)   The certificate of number and name of the vessel.
(4)   The name and address of the vessel owner or owners and the vessel operator.

(d)   If the operator of the vessel cannot give notice required by this section, each person on board the vessel shall notify the law enforcement agency or determine that notice has been given. Upon receiving notice under this section, a law enforcement agency shall immediately provide the Commission and the United States Coast Guard with the information required by this section. (1959, c. 1064, s. 11; 1999-248, s. 3; 2006-185, s. 1.)

§ 75A-12. Furnishing information to agency of United States.

In accordance with any request duly made by an authorized official or agency of the United States, any information compiled or otherwise available to the Commission pursuant to G.S. 75A-11(b) shall be transmitted to the requesting official or agency of the United States. (1959, c. 1064, s. 12; 2006-185, s. 1.)

§ 75A-13. Water skis, surfboards, etc.

(a)   No person shall operate a vessel on any water of this State for towing a person or persons on water skis, a surfboard, or similar device unless at least one of the following conditions is met:

    (1)   There is in the vessel a person, in addition to the operator, in a position to observe the progress of the person or persons being towed.

    (2)   The persons being towed wear a personal flotation device.

    (3)   The vessel is equipped with a rear view mirror.

(b)   No person shall operate a vessel on any water of this State towing a person or persons on water skis, a surfboard, or similar device, nor shall any person engage in water skiing, surfboarding, or similar activity at any time between the hours from one hour after sunset to one hour before sunrise.

(c)   The provisions of subsections (a) and (b) of this section do not apply to a performer engaged in a professional exhibition.

(d)   No person shall operate or manipulate any vessel, tow rope, or other device by which the direction or location of water skis, a surfboard, or similar device may be affected or controlled in such a way as to cause the water skis, surfboard, or similar device, or any person thereon to collide with any object or person. (1959, c. 1064, s. 13; 2006-185, s. 1.)

§ 75A-13.1. Skin and scuba divers.

(a)   No person shall engage in skin diving or scuba diving in the waters of this State that are open to boating, or assist in such diving, without displaying a diver's flag from a mast, buoy, or other structure at the place of diving; and no person shall display such flag except when diving operations are under way or in preparation.

(b)   The diver's flag shall be square, not less than 12 inches on a side, and shall be of red background with a diagonal white stripe, of a width equal to one fifth of the flag's height, running from the upper corner adjacent to the mast downward to the opposite outside corner.

(c)   No operator of a vessel under way in the waters of this State shall permit the vessel to approach closer than 50 feet to any structure from which a diver's flag is then being displayed, except where the flag is so positioned as to constitute an unreasonable obstruction to navigation; and no person shall engage in skin diving or scuba diving or display a diver's flag in any locality that will unreasonably obstruct vessels from making legitimate navigational use of the water.

(d)   A person who violates a provision of this section is responsible for an infraction as provided in G.S. 14-3.1. (1969, c. 97, s. 1; 2006-185, s. 1; 2013-360, s. 18B.15(b); 2013-380, s. 6.)

§ 75A-13.2: Repealed by Session Laws 1999-447, s. 3.

§ 75A-13.3. Personal watercraft.

(a)   No person shall operate a personal watercraft on the waters of this State at any time between sunset and sunrise. For purposes of this section, "personal watercraft" means a small vessel that uses an outboard or propeller-driven motor, or an inboard motor powering a water jet pump, as its primary source of motive power and which is designed to be operated by a person sitting, standing, or kneeling on, or being towed behind the vessel, rather than in the conventional manner of sitting or standing inside the vessel.

(a1)   No person shall operate a personal watercraft on the waters of this State at greater than no-wake speed within 100 feet of an anchored or moored vessel, a dock, pier, swim float, marked swimming area, swimmers, surfers, persons engaged in angling, or any manually operated propelled vessel, unless the personal watercraft is operating in a narrow channel. No person shall operate a personal watercraft in a narrow channel at greater than no-wake speed within 50 feet of an anchored or moored vessel, a dock, pier, swim float, marked swimming area, swimmers, surfers, persons engaged in angling, or any manually operated propelled vessel.

(b)   Except as otherwise provided in this subsection, no person under 16 years of age shall operate a personal watercraft on the waters of this State, and it is unlawful for the owner of a personal watercraft or a person who has temporary or permanent responsibility for a person under the age of 16 to knowingly allow that person to operate a personal watercraft. A person of at least 14 years of age but under 16 years of age may operate a personal watercraft on the waters of this State if:

(1) The person is accompanied by a person of at least 18 years of age who physically occupies the watercraft and who is in compliance with G.S. 75A-16.2; or

(2) The person (i) possesses on his or her person while operating the watercraft, identification showing proof of age and a boating safety certification card issued by the Commission, proof of other satisfactory completion of a boating safety education course approved by the National Association of State Boating Law Administrators (NASBLA), or proof of other boating safety education in compliance with G.S. 75A-16.2; and (ii) produces that identification and proof upon the request of an officer of the Commission or local law enforcement agency.

(b1) A person who is the lawful owner of a personal watercraft or a person having control of a personal watercraft who knowingly allows a person under 16 years of age to operate a personal watercraft in violation of the provisions of subsection (b) of this section is responsible for an infraction as provided in G.S. 14-3.1.

(c) No livery shall lease, hire, or rent a personal watercraft to or for operation by a person under 16 years of age, except as provided in subsection (b) of this section.

(c1) No person, firm, or corporation shall engage in the business of renting personal watercraft to the public for operation by the rentee unless the person, firm, or corporation has secured insurance for the liability of the person, firm, or corporation and that of the rentee, in such an amount as is hereinafter provided, from an insurance company duly authorized to sell liability insurance in this State. Each personal watercraft rented must be covered by a policy of liability insurance insuring the owner and rentee and their agents and employees while in the performance of their duties against loss from any liability imposed by law for damages including damages for care and loss of services because of bodily injury to or death of any person and injury to or destruction of property caused by accident arising out of the operation of such personal watercraft, subject to the following minimum limits: three hundred thousand dollars ($300,000) per occurrence.

(c2) A vessel livery that fails to carry liability insurance in violation of subsection (c1) of this section is guilty of a Class 2 misdemeanor and shall only be subject to a fine not to exceed one thousand dollars ($1,000).

(c3) A vessel livery shall provide the operator of a leased personal watercraft with basic safety instruction prior to allowing the operation of the leased personal watercraft. "Basic safety instruction" shall include direction on how to safely operate the personal watercraft and a review of the safety provisions of this section. A vessel livery that fails to provide basic safety instruction is responsible for an infraction as provided in G.S. 14-3.1.

(d) No person shall operate a personal watercraft on the waters of this State, nor shall the owner of a personal watercraft knowingly allow another person to operate that personal watercraft on the waters of this State, unless:

(1)   Each person riding on or being towed behind the vessel is wearing a type I, type II, type III, or type V personal flotation device approved by the United States Coast Guard. Inflatable personal flotation devices do not satisfy this requirement; and

(2)   In the case of a personal watercraft equipped by the manufacturer with a lanyard-type engine cut-off switch, the lanyard is securely attached to the person, clothing, or flotation device of the operator at all times while the personal watercraft is being operated in such a manner to turn off the engine if the operator dismounts while the watercraft is in operation.

(d1)   No person shall operate a personal watercraft towing another person on water skis, a surfboard, or similar device unless:

(1)   The personal watercraft has on board, in addition to the operator, an observer who shall monitor the progress of the person or persons being towed, or the personal watercraft is equipped with a rearview mirror; and

(2)   The total number of persons operating, observing, and being towed does not exceed the number of passengers identified by the manufacturer as the maximum safe load for the vessel.

(e)   A personal watercraft must at all times be operated in a reasonable and prudent manner. Maneuvers that endanger life, limb, or property shall constitute reckless operation of a vessel as provided in G.S. 75A-10, and include any of the following:

(1)   Unreasonably or unnecessarily weaving through congested vessel traffic.

(2)   Jumping the wake of another vessel within 100 feet of the other vessel or when visibility around the other vessel is obstructed.

(3)   Intentionally approaching another vessel in order to swerve at the last possible moment to avoid collision.

(4)   Repealed by Session Laws 2000-52, s. 2.

(5)   Operating contrary to the "rules of the road" or following too closely to another vessel, including another personal watercraft. For purposes of this subdivision, "following too closely" means proceeding in the same direction and operating at a speed in excess of 10 miles per hour when approaching within 100 feet to the rear or 50 feet to the side of another vessel that is underway unless that vessel is operating in a narrow channel, in which case a personal watercraft may operate at the speed and flow of other vessel traffic.

(f)   The provisions of this section do not apply to a performer engaged in a professional exhibition, a person or persons engaged in an activity authorized under G.S. 75A-14, or a person attempting to rescue another person who is in danger of losing life or limb.

(f1)   For purposes of this section, "narrow channel" means a segment of the waters of the State 300 feet or less in width.

(g)   Repealed by Session Laws 1999-447, s. 1.

(h)   Nothing in this section prohibits units of local government, marine commissions, or local lake authorities from regulating personal watercraft pursuant to the provisions of G.S. 160A-176.2 or any other law authorizing such regulation, provided that the regulations are more restrictive than the provisions of this section or regulate aspects of personal watercraft operation that are not covered by this section. Whenever a unit of local government, marine commission, or local lake authority regulates personal watercraft pursuant to this subsection, it shall conspicuously post signs that are reasonably calculated to provide notice to personal watercraft users of the stricter regulations. (1997-129, s. 1; 1999-447, s. 1; 2000-52, ss. 1-4; 2005-161, s. 1; 2006-185, s. 1; 2009-282, s. 2; 2013-360, s. 18B.15(c); 2013-380, ss. 7, 8.)

§ 75A-14: Repealed by Session Laws 1999-248, s. 4.

§ 75A-14.1. Lake Norman No-Wake Zone.

It is unlawful to operate a vessel at greater than no-wake speed within 50 yards of a vessel launching area, bridge, dock, pier, marina, vessel storage structure, or vessel service area on the waters of Lake Norman. (1997-129, s. 4; 1997-257, s. 10; 1998-217, s. 49; 2006-185, s. 1.)

§ 75A-14.2. Temporary waiver of enforcement of no-wake zones.

The Wildlife Resources Commission may temporarily and conditionally waive enforcement of a no-wake zone upon petition by a unit of local government that encompasses or abuts the no-wake zone if, after investigation of the reasons given for the temporary and conditional waiver, the Commission determines that public safety and the public welfare will not be significantly compromised by the waiver. (2007-46, s. 1.)

§ 75A-15. Rules on water safety; adoption of the United States Aids to Navigation System.

(a)   In accordance with subsection (b) of this section, the Commission is empowered to adopt rules, for the local water in question, as to:

    (1)   Operation of vessels, including restrictions concerning speed zones, and type of activity conducted.

    (2)   Promotion of boating and water safety generally by occupants of vessels, swimmers, fishermen, and others using the water.

    (3)   Placement and maintenance of navigation aids and markers, in conformity with governing provisions of law.

Prior to the adoption of any rules, the Commission shall investigate the water recreation and safety needs of the local water in question. In conducting the investigation, the Commission in its discretion may hold public hearings on the rules proposed and the general needs of the local water in question. After completion of the investigation and application of standards, the Commission may in its discretion adopt the rules requested, adopt them in an amended form, or refuse to adopt them. After adoption, the Commission may amend or repeal the rules after first holding a public hearing.

(b)   Any subdivision of this State may, but only after public notice, make formal application to the Commission for rules on waters within the subdivision's territorial limits as to the matters listed in subsection (a) of this section. The Commission may adopt rules applicable to local areas of water defined by the Commission that are found to be heavily used for water recreation purposes by persons from other areas of the State and as to which there is not coordinated local interest in regulation.

(b1)   The Commission may adopt rules to prohibit entry of vessels into public swimming areas and to establish speed zones at public vessel launching ramps, marinas, or vessel service areas and on other congested water areas where there are demonstrated water safety hazards. Enforcement of rules adopted pursuant to this subsection shall be dependent upon placement and maintenance of regulatory markers in accordance with the United States Aids to Navigation System by the Commission or an agency designated by the Commission.

(c)   The United States Aids to Navigation System, as established by 33 Code of Federal Regulations Part 62 (July 1, 2005 edition), is hereby adopted for use on the waters of North Carolina. The Commission is authorized to adopt rules implementing the marking system and may:

(1)   Modify provisions as necessary to meet the special water recreational and safety needs of this State, provided that the modifications do not depart in any essential manner from the uniform standards being adopted in other states.

(2)   Modify provisions as necessary to conform with amendments to the marking system that may be proposed for adoption by the states.

(3)   Enact supplementary standards regarding design, construction, placement, and maintenance of markers.

(4)   Enact clarifying rules as to matters not covered with precision in the United States Aids to Navigation System.

(5) Enact implementing rules as to matters left to State discretion in the United States Aids to Navigation System.

(6) Enact rules forbidding or restricting the placement of markers either throughout the State or in certain classes or areas of waters without prior permission having been obtained from the Commission or some agency or official designated by the Commission.

(c1) It is unlawful to place or maintain any marker of the sort covered by the marking system in the waters of North Carolina that does not conform to or is in violation of the marking system and the implementing rules of the Commission.

(d) Rules enacted under the authority of subsections (a), (b), and (b1) of this section shall supersede all local rules in conflict or incompatible with such rules. As used in this subsection, "local rules" shall include provisions relating to boating, water safety, or other recreational use of local waters in special local, or private acts, in ordinances or rules of local governing bodies, or in ordinances or rules of local water authorities. Except as may be authorized in subsections (a), (b), and (b1) of this section, no local rules may be made respecting the United States Aids to Navigation System and its implementation or respecting supplemental safety equipment on vessels.

(e) The Commission may adopt rules prohibiting entry or use by vessels or swimmers of waters of the State immediately surrounding impoundment structures and powerhouses associated with electric generating facilities that are found to pose a hazard to water safety. This subsection shall not apply to the Person-Caswell Lake Authority, Carolina Power and Light Company Lake (Hyco). (1959, c. 1064, s. 15; 1965, c. 394; 1969, c. 1093, s. 4; 1977,

c. 424; 1983 (Reg. Sess., 1984), c. 1082, ss. 4, 5; 1987, c. 827, s. 5; 1993 (Reg. Sess., 1994), c. 753, s. 3; 2006-185, s. 1.)

§ 75A-16. Repealed by Session Laws 1979, c. 830, s. 9, effective July 1, 1980.

§ 75A-16.1. Boating safety course.

(a)   The Commission shall institute and coordinate a statewide course of instruction in boating safety, and in so doing may cooperate with any political subdivision of the State or with any reputable organization having as one of its objectives the promotion of boating safety.

(b)   The Commission shall designate those persons or agencies authorized to conduct the course of instruction, and this designation shall be valid until revoked by the Commission. Within 30 days of completion of a course of instruction, a designated person or agency shall submit to the Commission a list of the names of all persons who successfully completed the course of instruction conducted by the designated person or agency.

(c)   The Commission may conduct the course in boating safety using Commission personnel or other persons at times or in areas in which competent agencies are unable or unwilling to meet the demand for instruction.

(d)   The Commission shall issue a boating safety certification card to each person who successfully completes the course of instruction.

(e)   The Commission shall adopt rules to provide for the course of instruction and the issuance of boating safety certification cards consistent with the purposes of this section.

(f)   Any person who presents a fictitious boating safety certification card or who attempts to obtain a boating safety certification card through fraud is guilty of a Class 2 misdemeanor. (2006-185, s. 1.)

§ 75A-16.2. Boating safety education required.

(a)   No person shall operate a vessel with a motor of 10 horsepower or greater on the public waters of this State unless the operator has met the requirements for boating safety education.

(b)   A person shall be considered in compliance with the requirements of boating safety education if the person does one of the following:

> (1)   Completes and passes the boating safety course instituted by the Wildlife Resources Commission under G.S. 75A-16.1 or another boating safety course that is approved by the National Association of State Boating Law Administrators (NASBLA) and accepted by the Wildlife Resources Commission;
>
> (2)   Passes a proctored equivalency examination that tests the knowledge of information included in the curriculum of an approved course;
>
> (3)   Possesses a valid or expired license to operate a vessel issued to maritime personnel by the United States Coast Guard;
>
> (4)   Possesses a State-approved nonrenewable temporary operator's certificate to operate a vessel for 90 days that was issued with the certificate of number for the vessel, if the boat was new or was sold with a transfer of ownership;
>
> (5)   Possesses a rental or lease agreement from a vessel rental or leasing business that lists the person as the authorized operator of the vessel;

(6)   Properly displays Commission-issued dealer registration numbers during the demonstration of the vessel;

(7)   Operates the vessel under onboard direct supervision of a person who is at least 18 years of age and who meets the requirements of this section;

(8)   Demonstrates that he or she is not a resident, is temporarily using the waters of this State for a period not to exceed 90 days, and meets any applicable boating safety education requirements of the state or nation of residency;

(9)   Has assumed operation of the vessel due to the illness or physical impairment of the initial operator, and is returning the vessel to shore in order to provide assistance or care for the operator;

(10)   Is registered as a commercial fisherman or a person who is under the onboard direct supervision of a commercial fisherman while operating the commercial fisherman's boat; or

(11)   Provides proof that he or she was born before January 1, 1988.

Any person who operates a vessel with a motor of 10 horsepower or greater on the waters of this State shall, upon the request of a law enforcement officer, present to the officer a certification card or proof that the person has complied with the provisions of this section.

(c)   Any person who violates a provision of this section or a rule adopted pursuant to this section is responsible for an infraction, as provided in G.S. 14-3.1, and shall pay a fine of fifty dollars ($50.00). A person may not be responsible for violating this section if the person produces in court at the adjudicatory hearing a certification card or proof that the person has completed and passed a boating safety course in compliance with subdivision (b)(1) of this section.

(d)   No unit of local government shall enact any ordinance or rule relating to boating safety education, and this law preempts all existing ordinances or rules.

(e)   An operator of a personal watercraft on the public waters of this State remains subject to any more specific provision of law found in G.S. 75A-13.3. (2009-282, s. 1; 2013-380, s. 9.)

§ 75A-17. Enforcement of Chapter.

(a)   Every wildlife protector and every other law-enforcement officer of this State and its subdivisions shall have the authority to enforce the provisions of this Chapter and in the exercise thereof shall have authority to stop any vessel subject to this Chapter. Wildlife protectors or other law enforcement officers of this State, after having identified themselves as law enforcement officers, shall have authority to board and inspect any vessel subject to this Chapter.

(b)   In order to secure broader enforcement of the provisions of this Chapter, the Commission is authorized to enter into an agreement with the Department of Environmental Quality whereby the enforcement personnel of the Department shall assume responsibility for enforcing the provisions of this Chapter in the territory and area normally policed by enforcement personnel of the Commission and whereby the Commission shall contribute a share of the expense of such personnel according to a ratio of time and effort expended by them in enforcing the provisions of this Chapter, when the ratio has been agreed upon by both of the contracting agencies. The agreement may be modified from time to time as conditions may warrant.

(c)   Law enforcement vessels may use a flashing blue light on the waters of this State whenever they are engaged in law enforcement or public safety activities. The use of a blue light by any other vessel is prohibited. A person other than a law enforcement officer who activates, installs, or operates a flashing blue light on a vessel other than a law enforcement vessel is guilty of a Class 1 misdemeanor.

(d)   A siren may not be used on any vessel other than an official law enforcement vessel or other official emergency response vessel.

(e)   Vessels operated on the waters of this State shall stop when directed to do so by a law enforcement officer. When stopped, vessels shall remain at idle speed, or shall maneuver in such a way as to permit the officer to come alongside the vessel. Law enforcement officers may direct vessels to stop by using a flashing blue light, a siren, or an oral command by officers in uniform. A person who violates this subsection is guilty of a Class 2 misdemeanor.

(f)   Vessels operated on the waters of this State shall slow to a no-wake speed when passing within 100 feet of a law enforcement vessel that is displaying a flashing blue light unless the vessel is in a narrow channel. Vessels operated on the waters of this State in a narrow channel shall slow to a no-wake speed when passing within 50 feet of a law enforcement vessel that is displaying a flashing blue light. A person who violates this subsection is responsible for an infraction as provided in G.S. 14-3.1. (1959, c. 1064, s. 17; 1965, c. 957, s. 9; 1973, c. 1262, ss. 28, 86; 1977, c. 771, s. 4; 1989, c. 727, s. 218(17); 1997-443, s. 11A.119(a); 2006-185, s. 1; 2013-360, s. 18B.15(d); 2015-241, s. 14.30(u).)

§ 75A-18. Penalties.

(a)   Except as otherwise provided, a person who violates a provision of this Article is responsible for an infraction as provided in G.S. 14-3.1. This limitation shall not apply in a case where a more severe penalty is prescribed in this Chapter.

(b)   through (e) Repealed by Session Laws 2006-185, s. 1.

(f)   Except as otherwise provided in this Chapter, a person who violates a rule adopted by the Commission under the authority of this Chapter is responsible for an infraction as provided in G.S. 14-3.1 and shall pay a fine of fifty dollars ($50.00). A person responsible for an infraction under this Chapter shall not be assessed court costs. (1959, c. 1064, s. 18; 1965, c. 634, s. 3; c. 793; 1969, c. 97, s. 2; 1979, c. 761, s. 8; 1985, c. 615, ss. 6, 7; 1989, c. 742, s. 2; 1993, c. 539, ss. 566, 1285; 1994, Ex. Sess., c. 24, s. 14(c); 1997-129, s. 3; 1999-447, s. 2; 2006-185, s. 1; 2013-360, s. 18B.15(e); 2013-380, s. 10.)

§ 75A-19. Operation of vessels by manufacturers, dealers, etc.

Notwithstanding any other provisions of this Chapter, the Commission may adopt rules regarding the operation of vessels by manufacturers, distributors, dealers, and demonstrators as the Commission may deem necessary and proper. (1959, c. 1064, s. 181/2; 2006-185, s. 1.)

Article 2. Local Water Safety Committees.

§§ 75A-20 through 75A-25. Repealed by Session Laws 1983 (Regular Session, 1984), c. 1082, s. 3, effective July 5, 1984.

§ 75A-26. Local water safety committees.

(a)   In order that responsible State and local officials may consult with an advisory body as to the needs and desires of the public in matters of water recreation and safety in various local waters, local authorities may sponsor local water safety committees. When a local government or two or more local governments acting jointly determine that the interests of the public would be served by sponsorship of a local water safety committee, such local government or governments may sponsor a committee. As used in this section, the noun "sponsor" shall include a sponsoring local government or a sponsoring group of local governments acting jointly.

(b)   Members of a local committee shall be selected by the sponsor to represent various viewpoints and interests respecting water recreation and safety in the locality concerned. The membership of the committee shall be not less than 15 nor more than 35, and members shall serve at the pleasure of the sponsor. Except where the charter granted by the sponsor may make specific provision, the members of a local committee shall select their officers, determine the need for subcommittees (if any), provide for times and places of regular meetings, and otherwise order the internal organization and administration of the committee. Special meetings may be held:

    (1)   Upon the call of such officers or members of the local committee as may be specified in the charter from the sponsor or the bylaws enacted by the committee.

    (2)   Upon the call of three members of the governing body or bodies of the sponsor.

    (3)   Upon the call of the chairman of the North Carolina Water Safety Committee.

(c)	Where the sponsor finds that an existing organization or committee is sufficiently broadly based to represent the various community interests, it may sponsor (and at any time withdraw sponsorship of) the activities of such organization or committee relating to water recreation and safety in lieu of creating a separate local committee. In the event an existing organization or committee is sponsored, the membership restrictions of subsection (b) do not apply. The phrase "local committee" as used in this section shall include such sponsored existing organizations and committees as well as separate committees.

(d)	Except as indicated below, members of a local committee shall serve without compensation from the sponsor. Public officers and employees who are acting within the scope and course of their employment, however, may receive such travel and subsistence allowance as authorized by law when attending meetings, whether as members or observers, or otherwise assisting or participating in the affairs of a local committee. Within the bounds set by governing provisions of the law generally, a sponsor may also provide administrative and staff services to a local committee and may underwrite or finance its projects which are carried out to the benefit of water recreation and safety in the area concerned.

(e)	At the time of sponsorship, or withdrawal of sponsorship, of a local committee, the sponsor shall notify the following persons of the action taken:
    (1)	The chairman of the North Carolina Water Safety Committee.
    (2)	The Executive Director of the North Carolina Wildlife Resources Commission.

(f)	All meetings of separately created local committees shall be open to the public. Where an existing organization or committee has received sponsorship, all its meetings devoted to carrying out the advisory functions of a local committee shall be open to the public.

    (g)   Members of a local committee are under an obligation:

        (1)   To keep themselves informed as to problems of water recreation and safety in their area.

        (2)   To study such problems concerning water recreation and safety as may be referred to them by their sponsor or by the chairman of the North Carolina Water Safety Committee.

        (3)   To make reports from time to time, either on their own motion or in response to a request for a study, on problems of water recreation and safety, and with suggestions for remedies where such are indicated and feasible. Such reports may be made to the sponsor, the chairman of the North Carolina Water Safety Committee, the Executive Director of the North Carolina Wildlife Resources Commission, or any other public or private person, agency, firm, corporation, or organization with the power to effect improvements in the level of water recreation and safety available to the public.

        (4)   To take part in and, where necessary, to help coordinate programs of public education in the field of water safety. (1969, c. 1093, s. 3.)

Article 3. Boat Hull Anti-Copying Act.

§ 75A-27 through 75A-31: Repealed by Session Laws 1991, c. 191, s. 1.

Article 4. Vessel Titling Act.

§ 75A-32. Short title.

This Article shall be known as the Vessel Titling Act. (1989, c. 739, s. 1; 2006-185, s. 2.)

§ 75A-33. Definitions.

The definitions set forth in G.S. 75A-2 shall apply to this Article, unless the context clearly requires a different meaning. (1989, c. 739, s. 1; 2006-185, s. 2.)

§ 75A-34. Who may apply for certificate of title; authority of employees of Commission.

(a)   Any owner of a motorized vessel or sailboat 14 feet or longer or any personal watercraft, as defined in G.S. 75A-13.3(a), that is applying for a certificate of number for the first time in this State pursuant to G.S. 75A-5(a), and any new owner of a motorized vessel or sailboat 14 feet or longer or any personal watercraft to whom ownership is being transferred under G.S. 75A-5(c) shall apply to the Commission for a certificate of title for that vessel. Any other vessel may be titled in this State at the owner's option. A vessel may not be titled in this State if it is titled in another state, unless the current title is surrendered along with the application for a certificate of title in this State. The

Commission shall issue a certificate of title upon reasonable evidence of ownership, which may be established by affidavit, bill of sale, manufacturer's statement of origin, certificate of title in this State, certificate of number or title from another state, or other document satisfactory to the Commission. Only one certificate of title may be issued for any vessel in this State. A vessel may not be titled in this State if it is documented with the United States Coast Guard, unless the documentation has expired or been deleted by the United States Coast Guard. The Commission shall issue a certificate of title upon receipt of a completed application, along with the appropriate fee and reasonable evidence of ownership. The Commission shall require a manufacturer's statement of origin for all new vessels being issued a certificate of number and a certificate of title for the first time. The Commission may request a pencil tracing of the hull identification number (serial number) for vessels being transferred, in order to positively identify the vessel before issuance of a certificate of title for that vessel.

(b)   Employees of the Commission are vested with the power to administer oaths and to take acknowledgements and affidavits incidental to the administration and enforcement of this section. They shall receive no compensation for these services. (1989, c. 739, s. 1; 2006-185, s. 2; 2013-360, s. 14.22(e).)

§ 75A-35. Form and contents of application.

(a)   The owner or the owner's attorney shall apply for a certificate of title for a vessel. The application shall contain the name, residence, and mailing address of the owner, the county where the vessel is taxed, proof of ownership, and a statement of all liens or encumbrances upon the vessel in the order of their priority. The application shall also contain the names and addresses of all persons having any interest in the vessel.

(b)   Every application for a certificate of title for a vessel shall contain a brief description of the vessel to be titled, including the name of the manufacturer, certificate of number, hull identification number, length, type, and principal material of construction, model year, and purchase information. It shall also include the name and address of the previous owner or owners from whom the vessel was obtained. If the vessel has an outboard motor of greater than 25 horsepower, the application shall also contain identification of the motor, including the serial number and manufacturer. The application shall be made on forms prescribed and furnished by the Commission and shall contain other information as may be required by the Commission. (1989, c. 739, s. 1; 2006-185, s. 2.)

§ 75A-36. Notice by owner of change of address.

Whenever any person, after applying for or obtaining the certificate of title of a vessel, moves from the address shown on the application or certificate of title, that person shall, within 30 days of moving, notify the Commission of the change of address on a form acceptable to the Commission. (1989, c. 739, s. 1; 2006-185, s. 2.)

§ 75A-37. Certificate of title as evidence; duration; transfer of title.

(a)   A certificate of title is prima facie evidence of the ownership of a vessel. A certificate of title shall remain in force for the life of the vessel.

(b)   Upon the sale, assignment, or transfer of a vessel for which a certificate of title has been issued under this Article, the legal holder of the certificate of title shall deliver it to the purchaser or transferee. The assignment on the certificate must be completed showing transfer of ownership to the purchaser or transferee and settlement of all outstanding liens and encumbrances. The new owner shall submit the assigned certificate of title to the Commission, accompanied by evidence satisfactory to the Commission that all outstanding liens have been released, with the application for transfer of title. The application shall contain all the information required by the Commission for the transfer in order to identify the vessel and the new owner. The application shall show any and all new liens and encumbrances on the vessel, in order of priority, incurred by the owner. The nature of the new liens and encumbrances shall also be given, along with the name and address of all secured parties. (1989, c. 739, s. 1; 2006-185, s. 2.)

§ 75A-38. Commission's records; fees.

(a)   The Commission shall maintain a record of any title it issues.

(b)   The Commission shall charge a fee of thirty dollars ($30.00) to issue a new or transfer certificate of title. The Commission shall transfer on a quarterly basis at least ten dollars ($10.00) of each new or transfer certificate of title to the Shallow Draft Navigation Channel Dredging and Aquatic Weed Fund established by G.S. 143-215.73F. The Commission shall charge a fee of ten dollars ($10.00) for each duplicate title it issues and for the recording of a supplemental lien. (1989, c. 739, s. 1; 2006-185, s. 2; 2013-360, s. 14.22(f); 2014-100, s. 14.19(c); 2016-94, s. 14.12(c).)

§ 75A-39. Duplicate certificate of title.

The Commission may issue a duplicate certificate of title plainly marked "duplicate" across its face upon application by the person entitled to hold the certificate if the Commission is satisfied that the original certificate has been lost, stolen, mutilated, destroyed, or has become illegible. Mutilated or illegible certificates shall be returned to the Commission with the application for a duplicate. If a duplicate certificate of title has been issued and the lost or stolen original is recovered, the original shall be promptly surrendered to the Commission. A duplicate certificate of title, not bearing the word "duplicate" across its face, shall be issued for anyone having an address change or name change so long as the original title is surrendered and the appropriate fees paid as provided in G.S. 75A-38(b). If the original certificate of title is not surrendered to the Commission, the duplicate certificate of title shall be plainly marked "duplicate" across its face. (1989, c. 739, s. 1; 2006-185, s. 2.)

§ 75A-40. Certificate to show security interests.

The Commission, after receiving an application for a certificate of title for a vessel, shall, upon issuing the certificate of title to the owner, show upon the face of the certificate of title all security interests in the order of their priority as shown in the application. (1989, c. 739, s. 1; 2006-185, s. 2.)

§ 75A-41. Security interests subsequently created.

Except for security interests in vessels that are inventory held for sale, security interests created in vessels by the voluntary act of the owner after the original issue of title to the owner must be shown on the certificate of title. In such cases, the owner shall file an application with the Commission on a form furnished for that purpose, setting forth all security interests and other information as the Commission requires. The Commission, if satisfied that it is proper that the security interests be recorded, shall upon surrender of the certificate of title covering the vessel, issue a new certificate of title showing any security interests in the order of the priority according to the date of the filing of the application. For the purpose of recording the subsequent security interest, the Commission may require any secured party to deliver the certificate of title to the Commission. The newly issued certificate shall be sent or delivered to the secured party of first priority listed on the certificate of title. (1989, c. 739, s. 1; 2000-169, s. 38; 2006-185, s. 2.)

§ 75A-42. Certificate as notice of security interest.

A certificate of title, when issued by the Commission showing a security interest, shall be deemed adequate notice to the State, creditors, and purchasers that a security interest in the vessel exists. No other recording or filing of the creation or reservation of a security interest in the county or city wherein the purchaser or debtor resides or elsewhere is necessary and shall not be required. Vessels, other than those that are inventory held for sale, for which a certificate of title is currently in effect, shall be exempt from the provisions of G.S. 25-9-309, 25-9-310, 25-9-312, 25-9-320, 25-9-322, 25-9-323, 25-9-324, 25-9-331, 25-9-404, 25-9-405, 25-9-406, and 25-9-501 to 25-9-526 for so long as the certificate of title remains in effect. (1989, c. 739, s.1; 2000-169, s. 39; 2006-185, s. 2.)

§ 75A-43. Security interest may be filed within 30 days after purchase.

If application for the recordation of a security interest to be placed upon a vessel is filed in the principal office of the Commission within 30 days from the date of the applicant's purchase of the vessel, it shall be valid to all persons, including the State, as if the recordation had been done on the day the security interest was acquired. (1989, c. 739, s. 1; 2006-185, s. 2.)

§ 75A-44. Priority of security interests shown on certificates.

Except for security interests in vessels that are inventory held for sale, security interests shown upon the certificates of title issued by the Commission pursuant to applications for certificates shall have priority over any other liens or security interests against the vessel however created and recorded, except for a mechanics lien for repairs, provided that the mechanic furnishes the holder of any recorded lien who may request it with an itemized sworn statement of the work done and materials supplied for which the lien is claimed. (1989, c. 739, s.1; 2000-169, s. 40; 2006-185, s. 2.)

§ 75A-45. Legal holder of certificate of title subject to security interest.

The certificate of title of a vessel shall be delivered to the person holding the security interest having first priority upon the vessel and retained by that person until the entire amount of the security interest is fully paid by the owner of the vessel. The certificate of title shall then be delivered to the secured party next in order of priority and so on, or, if none, then to the owner of the vessel. (1989, c. 739, s. 1; 2006-185, s. 2.)

§ 75A-46. Release of security interest shown on certificate of title.

An owner, upon securing the release of any security interest upon a vessel shown upon the certificate of title issued for the vessel, may exhibit the documents evidencing the release, signed by the person or persons making the release, and the certificate of title to the Commission. When it is impossible to secure the release from the secured party, the owner may exhibit to the Commission any available evidence showing that the debt secured has been satisfied, together with a statement by the owner under oath that the debt has been paid. If the Commission determines that the secured debt has been satisfied in full, the Commission shall issue to the owner either a new certificate of title in proper form or an endorsement or rider showing the release of the security interest which the Commission shall attach to the outstanding certificate of title. (1989, c. 739, s. 1; 2006-185, s. 2.)

§ 75A-47. Surrender of certificate required when security interest paid.

It is unlawful and constitutes a Class 1 misdemeanor for a secured party who holds a certificate of title as provided in this Article to refuse or fail to surrender the certificate of title to the person legally entitled to it within 10 days after the security interest has been paid and satisfied. (1989, c. 739, s. 1; 1993, c. 539, s. 567; 1994, Ex. Sess., c. 24, s. 14(c); 2006-185, s. 2.)

§ 75A-48. Levy of execution, etc.

A levy made by virtue of an execution or other proper court order, upon a vessel for which a certificate of title has been issued by the Commission, shall constitute a lien, subsequent to security interests previously recorded by the Commission and subsequent to security interests in inventory held for sale and perfected as otherwise permitted by law, if and when the officer making the levy reports to the Commission at its principal office, on forms provided by the Commission, that the levy has been made and that the vessel levied upon has been seized by and is in the custody of the officer. Should the lien thereafter be satisfied or should the vessel levied upon and seized thereafter be released by the officer, the officer shall immediately report that fact to the Commission at its principal office. After a levy and seizure by an officer and before the officer reports the levy and seizure to the Commission, any person who fraudulently assigns, transfers, causes the certificate of title to be assigned or transferred, or causes a security interest to be shown upon the certificate of title, is guilty of a Class 1 misdemeanor. (1989, c. 739, s. 1; 1993, c. 539, s. 568; 1994, Ex. Sess., c. 24, s. 14(c); 2006-185, s. 2.)

§ 75A-49. Registration prima facie evidence of ownership; rebuttal.

A valid certificate of number issued under the provisions of this Chapter, or any similar document issued under the jurisdiction of any other state or country, shall be prima facie evidence of ownership of a vessel and entitlement to a certificate of title under the provisions of this Article, but ownership established by such documents shall be subject to rebuttal. (1989, c. 739, s. 1; 2006-185, s. 2.)